NECK-VERSE

Neck-Verse

U.A. FANTHORPE

PETERLOO POETS

First published in 1992
by Peterloo Poets
2 Kelly Gardens, Calstock, Cornwall PL18 9SA, U.K.

© 1992 by U.A. Fanthorpe

Reprinted 1999

**A catalogue record for this book is available
from the British Library**

ISBN 1–871471–33–8

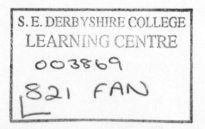

Printed in Great Britain by
Antony Rowe Ltd, Chippenham, Wiltshire

ACKNOWLEDGEMENTS are due to the editors of the following journals and anthologies: *Antaeus, Bête Noire, The Bristol Tryptich, Country Living, Druridge Bay Appeal, First and Always, Home and Away, Neighbours, Poetry Book Society Anthology (1989–90), Poetry Now, Poetry Review, Stand.*

For Rosemarie Bailey
(and in memory of Vera Bailey)

Contents

As well as the Bible and Shakespeare ... ?

You are what   I would choose

for companion in the desert.
You would know the way out,
think providently about water.

in the solicitor's office.
You would have generous answers
for disagreeable contingencies.

on the motorway.
In your presence
I shouldn't notice tailbacks.

at the picnic.
You would have remembered matches,
have brought a surprise for the greedy.

at the funeral.
You would speak gently with mourners,
but your hands would be warm with life.

After Reading Anita Brookner

Here, the painter thought,
Bearing in mind her social class,
Her husband's income, angle of the light,
Presence of offspring, dogs, various trees,
Husband, of course—and he upon her left,
She leaning on his arm—yes, here, just here,
I'll have the lady.

                              Cramped centuries later
She risks a foot outside the frame.

Brauneberg on the River Mosel

A place born with a vocation
Should accept with grace, and not be curious.

Long-headed Romans recognised the gift:
Earth, water, wood, fire, frost and dawdling spring.

Since then names repetitive as a stammer
Have done the right things at the proper seasons,

Laid down now in their vaults under marigold and fuschia,
Licht, Zimmer, Boujong, Link. Not families, but years,

The human vintage. These bodies knew their uses:
Bend forward to dig, to harvest; lean back to swallow, to sing.

It is as easy as being a cat. A young one
Comes socially towards me, purring in German.

Perhaps he is of Roman descent; he seems untroubled
By my accent. We are person and cat. He has lemon eyes.

Yes, there is evil around. Weather is always chancy,
And blight of various sorts. The heirs

Are called away to die in other vineyards.
But endurance is here. Vocation demands it.

The mystery continues like the cat's descent,
The neatly decanted dead, the know-all river.

Back to the Front

I remember too much here. Michaelmas daisies
Butterfly-bushed in September; ceanothus
That got above itself; the derelict caravan
Where I ate cheese and wrote on used paper.
A scorched-earth policy has scotched the lot.

Instead there are new toys, compact, intense,
User-unfriendly. The photocopier will mug me
If I face it alone. The phone is tapped
By a sharp inquisitor, who calculates my fear.
This wallpaper, with its lilt of country kitchens,
Was chosen to deceive.

O you haven't changed! say the ones who knew me
(Wanting not to have changed themselves).
But I have. I am older and more frightened.
Sophisticated engines run free in the kitchen,
Only the patients still huddle and fumble, and somewhere
Someone is still screaming.

And I ought to have been here yesterday,
They tell me, for six-foot Laura's language.
Words Averil had never heard before . . . We had to explain them.
The police had to come. *Yes,* they say, *yes,*
You would have enjoyed yesterday.

(Would I have ever enjoyed yesterday? Was I,
Before I went away, so good at relishing
The anger of the helpless, such an eaves-dropper
On misery? I suppose I was. I suppose that
Was how I lived, semi-attached to despair.)

And still unspoken misery slams through
Prim clinical diction. Doctors alone are still
The privileged, who *think* or *say*; patients
Are back at their old tricks, *claiming*,
Admitting, denying. Still they endure urinary urgency,
Demonstrate gait disturbance, suffer
Massive insults to the brain.

Saddest of all, the one who should remember;
The smart young man, always in and out of good jobs,
With his cavalier lovelocks, his way with women,
Slow, now, and spoiled. He doesn't like the shape
Of twenty-pence pieces. Can I change them for him?
I don't like the shape of your future, Tony.
No magician here can change the currency,
Or the fused charge in your head.

Children Imagining a Hospital

for Kingswood County Primary School

I would like kindness, assurance,
A wide selection of books;
Lots of visitors, and a friend
To come and see me:
A bed by the window so I could look at
All the trees and fields, where I could go for a walk.
I'd like a hospital with popcorn to eat.
A place where I have my own way.

I would like HTV all to myself
And people bringing tea round on trollies;
Plenty of presents and plenty of cards
(I would like presents of food).
Things on the walls, like pictures, and things
That hang from the ceiling;
Long corridors to whizz down in wheelchairs.
Not to be left alone.

Clerical Error

My raiment stinks of the poor and the afflicted,
Of those whom healers, in a parody of you,
Have called back to mimic life.

I understand they are yours, and concern
All of us. But I am paid to do other things.
What must I do when Job and his daughters

Cram into my office where they are not allowed,
When I am typing medical reports against the clock,
When they mop and mow at me, seeking comfort?

I can tell you what I do. I address them as *love*
(Which is an insult), and say in a special soothing voice
(Which fools no one), *Go to the nurses, Judith,*

Judith, the nurses are looking for you (which is a lie).
How, Sir, am I to reconcile this with your clear
Instructions on dealing with the afflicted

And the poor? I do not seek to justify
My jobdescription. I did not write it,
But I volunteered to live by its commandments.

The Comforters

(for Philip Gross)

'The night cometh, when no man can work' (John, 9.iv)

Because their aim was not comfort, these
Are the comforters. That we find comfort
In what they wrote is our affair,
Not theirs. They never imagined immortality,
But watched each minute instant so hard
That it broke and flowered into ever.

Samuel of London, Gilbert of Selborne,
Francis of Clyro. And many more. Their own lives
By no means easy. We could tell them
The last dates in those diaries,
The hard labour of their dying: *a nest*
Of no less than seven stones in the left kidney;
A nervous cough and a wandering gout;
Peritonitis on a delayed, delightful
Honeymoon, aged thirty-nine.

                    We prize them
Not for their ends, but for the light
Of their everlasting present. Like them, we wait
For our own particular doomsday. Ours
May be premature, comprehensive. In the meantime, they
Reach down centuries with their accidental
Offer of comfort.

                 So I choose to believe
The old lie: that we all died normally
Ever after: *suddenly, following*
A road accident; after a long illness
Patiently borne. Not in the monstrous
Nuclear glare, but in the moderate
Darkness and light, darkness and light
That were the evening and the morning
Of the first ever day.

Costa Geriatrica

Evening quarters; land
Of the tranquil solo deckchair,
Of the early Ovaltine nightcap.

Here patient shop-assistants
Pick the right change from freckled
Trembling hands, and wrap

Single rashers tenderly. Here gardening
Is dangerous as bull-fights.
Dogs are dwarfish,

Coddled and lethal.
Here sagas are recited
Of long-dead husbands,

Varicose veins, comforting ministers,
Scarcity of large-print library books,
And endless hands of photographs

Of the happily-ever-after children
They make believe they have:
A nice son in the police force

And two lovely children.
Marriages are made in heaven,
For Mr Right not only exists

But arrives on cue. Tragedy
Is reduced to a foot-note: *The husband?*
Oh, he went wrong, or died,

Or something. They have all
Had what they wanted:
A lovely little square family,

And now, comforting morticians:
That's the man I want at my funeral,
If anything ever happens to me.

Dear Sir

(in memory of Dr H.J. Crow)

Body prescribed a comic part for you,
Denied the pallor of those inchless, touchy men
Who terrorise worlds into taking them seriously,

Refused too the surgeon's histrionic profile,
Noble silver forelock, hairless fiddler's fingers.
Made you a shy Scot, haggis-shaped.

Laughter skirts the need for small-talk,
So you made yourself droll. Materialised
Tiptoeing round corners as Quack-in-the-box

(*Aha! Gotcher!*), short stout explosion
Cued to blast off in muffled thuds of laughter,
Your warning note down corridors a drone.

Gracefully at Christmas you accepted your vocation,
Assumed kilt, sporran, funny hat, the lot.
Little Lord Mis-Rule, whose considerate war-whoops

Shrouded your morbid clinical conscience.

But Sir, I accuse you of worrying about patients
After hours; of not sleeping; of irrational fears
For your children; of concealing your DFC courage;
Of inconspicuous valour on behalf of underdogs;
Of exploring humanity's dark places,
And not letting on; of making us all believe
We were curable; of mixing the genres,
Of playing Quixote in Sancho Panza's clothes.

And, Sir, I accuse you of losing heart,
Of not curing that endless queue of incurables,
Blight of Thursday afternoons; of believing they'd vanish
If you shut your eyes and wished.

O Sir, I accuse you of dying at home,
In bed, asleep, without a hint of impaired
Cortical integrity; of failing to present
An interesting case; of leaving no heir
To that florid prose style, to that susceptibility
To *Limehouse Blues* late on Fridays
In a subordinate's subtle hum.

                              Dear Sir,
I accuse you of being irreplaceable. By God,
You had a crack at those windmills!

Descent

Some unremembered ancestor handed down to me
The practice of walking in darkness.

I didn't ask for it. I didn't want it.
Would choose to be without, if choice could move

The hard *fiat* of genes. I don't like darkness,
Its arbitrary swoops of stairs, its tunnel vaults,

Black bristly air, its emptiness. Others speak
Of the shining end of the tunnel. I haven't seen it.

This is my black. I alone
Am the authority, and I know no further

Than I've got, if that be anywhere.
I inherited no maps. A feckless line.

So I choose you, intransigent old Roman,
As ancestor; who, at the City's

Most sinister hour, fathomed the riddle;
Who faced the *it*; who, a man in arms and mounted,

Willingly entered the dark; who worked, however blindly,
However strangely, for good, under the earth. Who worked.

'Old Roman': Mettus Curtius. In BC 362 the earth in the Roman forum gave
way. A chasm appeared, and soothsayers said it could only be filled by throwing
in the city's greatest treasure. Mettus Curtius armed himself, mounted his horse,
and leaped in. The earth closed over him.

Dictator

He bestrides the wall-to-wall carpeting
Like a colossus. Imperiously
He surges from comma to semicolon.

Swaying in the throes of his passionate
Dictation, he creates little draughts,
Which stir my piles of flimsy paper.

If my phone rings, he answers
In an assumed accent.

Flexing the muscles of his mind,
He rides in triumph through the agendas
Of Area and District Management Committees,

Aborting all opposition with the flick
Of a fullstop. Laurelled and glossy,
He paces the colonnades of an imperial future,
With all his enemies liquidated.

When his letters are typed, he forgets to sign them.

Diglis Lock

Image of something unknown: dank walls
Where nothing grows but chains; moody
Unreadable water; dog howling near;
Keeper unseen; but we are scrutinised
From above. Then the great gates open
To let us through, and in the half-darkness
I hardly see you, but I know you are smiling.

Doubles

Since they're not made to tell truth,
They tell it squintingly. But tell it
They do. Curious beauty's mirror shows her
What the cameraman will never let fans see:
The dark side of the moon.

Light bends in its tracks, and the incompetent
Eye in its orbit walks upside down.

Inside the tunnel the traveller meets
Self not the same in the shadow that mimics
His place in the carriage. Those blurred angles
Are his double, waiting in the wings
Of a parallel but unscheduled journey.

North and south under the great mountains
Lights fizz, picks ferret, men fumble
In the random dark. First they will hear,
Then see, finally touch. *Is that you, brother?* they will say
In a different language.

Dumb Show

Freesias are such badly orchestrated flowers,
Dear mother-in-law, whom I may not call
Mother-in-law. The flowers succeed each other,
And when the first limp head spells *death*
I want to compost the lot. You innocently say
There's so much still to come. There is.
I prise from their green sockets
The moribund daily, severely. How should you know
What it is I remember, who gave me these flowers
When she went away, and I, to keep her close,
Endlessly doctored stalks? Fit emblem of a friendship
I wanted to be love, and made drag on
Until its florist's gleam was mildewed, rotten.

       At ninety-two,
You have your reasons too for keeping flowers
Beyond their common span.

Elegy for a Cat

'Cats being the least moveable of all animals because of their strong local
predilections; they are indeed in a domesticated state the serfs of the animal
creation, and properly attached to the soil.'
Southey: *Memoir of the Cats of Greta Hall*

Yours was the needlework, precise and painful
As claws on a loved naked shoulder, that sewed us
Back into that Merthyr morning, when, terrorised by toddlers,
You mined under our alien gateway, claimed sanctuary
In a jacket pocket.

You were the first to join our outlandish outfit
On that hilltop housing estate, with the garage-in-name-only,
Invisible agog neighbours, rhubarb corms from Aberfan;
You the first source of our logged jokes, with
Yours ears akimbo,

Eyes so excited they retreated behind their withers,
Living a paw-to-mouth existence, elbowing your way
Up bodies like a midshipman up rigging,
Your whiskers wet with passion, sitting with one ear
In a human mouth, to keep warm.

I was never sure that English was your language,
Though you were probably just as dim in Welsh,
Vague about status, doglike coming to a whistle,
Running on white bandy-legs with a
Welcoming cluck.

You never took offence, were always ready
With an Eskimo kiss of your pink plebeian nose;
Set records for slow learning when we installed
The cat-flap; had no idea of the gravitas
Proper to cats.

Exiled in Gloucestershire, you domesticated
It for us, materialised on preoccupied laps, and,
Mozart-addict, rushed in filthy-footed from
Uprooting lupins, to settle yourself round Primo's collar
When duets began.

Now the heir's installed, she colonises
The outposts (both next-doors, and one further)
Where she's feasted and fêted. Such cunning
Is natural to your prudent race, in case
Of catastrophe,

And I see, dear dead one, how we severed you
From your own earth, how you chose us to be
Your territory. You are there quite often,
Dear tabby blur, in my bad eye's corner. We left you
Nothing to haunt but ourselves.

Haunt us still, dear first-footer,
First to live with us, first to confirm
Us as livers-together, you who took us so simply
For granted, translator of life into
The vernacular of love.

You who saw love, where innocent others
Saw only convenience.

Escaping

You were the reader in the family,
Leading me on, through Pooh and Pimpernel,
To Swallows, Amazons, men in boats.

A good pupil, I devoured
My volume a day, *Willows* to *Wuthering*,
Enlisted at the public library, grew

Up to despise your straighbat lending
Library world, where quiet women in cardigans,
Prey to your serious charm, smuggled you

The latest of *your sort*. Thirty years later
I rumble at last your quirky taste
For quiet workers who one day absent-mindedly

Walk out of offices and discover
England. Was this your secret, surfacing only
In books we didn't discuss? While you waited

For death in Worthing, condescendingly I
Played the system for you, collected the ripping
Good yarns by gentlemanly pen-names —

Taffrail, Sapper, Bartimaeus—but drew
My sanctimonious teenage line at Ian Fleming.
Tell me, father, why you chose him for deathbed reading?

And tell me, did you want to walk out of our world?

Explorer

Chooses somewhere unexplored.
Goes without gear, walks alone
into the whiteout. Storm drones
in her head, hoods her, sticks to
her fingers. At her last ditch,
in the eye of despair, when
blizzard encompasses, a
blur, a brief silence, she is
there. Authorities after
will tell her where she was,
what she did. She has turned
her back on that, needs now
another place,
another way of going.

Familiars

There are two of them. The one that thinks it's a cat
comes at me widdershins, out of the dark,
inches along my spine, claw by implacable claw,
knots itself round my neck, croons in my ear
of things done wrong, of things bound to go wrong,
of the four last things. Seduced by its attentions,
its intimacy, its hoarse plausible cry,
I submit to darkness.

The other's imaginary too. It runs ahead,
as dogs do, stopping sometimes
to check on me. It would like me to throw sticks,
to give it a name. If I did, it would come at my call.
It rubs its silly head against my knees.
Almost I think it loves me,
would show me the way out. I haven't yet decided
what colour it shall be.

Going Under

I turn over pages, you say,
Louder than any woman in Europe.

But reading's my specific for keeping
Reality at bay; my lullaby.

You slip into sleep as fast
And neat as a dipper.
You lie there breathing, breathing.

My language is turn over
Over and over again. I am a fish
Netted on a giveaway mattress,
Urgent to be out of the air.

Reading would help; or pills.
But light would wake you from your resolute
Progress through night.

The dreams waiting for me twitter and bleat.
All the things I ever did wrong
Queue by the bed in order of precedence,
Worst last.

Exhausted by guilt, I nuzzle
Your shoulder. Out lobs
A casual, heavy arm. You anchor me
In your own easy sound.

Half-past Two

Once upon a schooltime
He did Something Very Wrong
(I forget what it was).

And She said he'd done
Something Very Wrong, and must
Stay in the school-room till half-past two.

(Being cross, she'd forgotten
She hadn't taught him Time.
He was too scared at being wicked to remind her.)

He knew a lot of time: he knew
Gettinguptime, timeyouwereofftime,
Timetogohomenowtime, TVtime,

Timeformykisstime (that was Grantime).
All the important times he knew,
But not half-past two.

He knew the clockface, the little eyes
And two long legs for walking,
But he couldn't click its language,

So he waited, beyond onceupona,
Out of reach of all the timefors,
And knew he'd escaped for ever

Into the smell of old chrysanthemums on Her desk,
Into the silent noise his hangnail made,
Into the air outside the window, into ever.

And then, *My goodness*, she said,
Scuttling in, *I forgot all about you.*
Run along or you'll be late.

So she slotted him back into schooltime,
And he got home in time for teatime,
Nexttime, notimeforthatnowtime,

But he never forgot how once by not knowing time,
He escaped into the clockless land for ever,
Where time hides tick-less waiting to be born.

Idyll

Not knowing even that we're on the way,
Until suddenly we're there. How shall we know?

There will be blackbirds, in a late March evening,
Blur of woodsmoke, whisky in grand glasses,

A poem of yours, waiting to be read; and one of mine;
A reflective bitch, a cat materialised

On a knee. All fears of present and future
Will be over, all guilts forgiven.

Maybe, heaven. Or maybe
We can get so far in this world. I'll believe we can.

King Edward's Flora

Your mind commandeers an island.
It seems simple. The neighbours
Are fish, not Christian fretful kings.

But in my halflight rear hulking trees,
Sulky, indigenous. Their names crack
Like an enemy's laugh. Short words, long trees.

It is not simple, cousin. I am the heir.
In me shines the clear claim of Wessex.
But the trees were before. Their roots run back

Below Grendel's forest. Ash was earliest.
Odin carved man from him; then alder,
The spirit tree, whose blood breaks red

Like ours. Alder is old. And guilty aspen,
Our Saviour's hangman, that chronicles Calvary
By a fine tremor in sweet summer air.

Then the holy ones: oak, many-fingered;
Holly, that fights for us against darkness,
And never fades; holy thorn that is quick

In the dead of the year, at birth-time; yew
Slow and sacred, that nothing grows under;
Red-berried rowan, that warns off witches.

Cut-and-come again bushes, hazel and willow;
And walnut the wanderer, tramping north
In the legions' brown fists.

All the bright welter of things
That maim, detain, deceive: bramble and briar,
Furze, moss, reed, rush, sedge; thistle the spearman.

These are my shieldwall. Take them, cousin,
You or Harold. Settle it between you,
For I choose ending: Edward the heirless,

My children the stone forest
At the West Minster. These are the trees
That I make holy. You, I can see,

Will be William of the Wastes.
My woods will not content you.

But take care, cousin. Trees are unchancy.
I say more than I know, being the last—
Son of Bad Counsel, Edward the healer—

You will plant your dynasty, if Harold lets you,
But the trees will not endure it. Your saplings totter
Under my trees. A red man sprawls, a white ship founders.

The boy from the gorse-bush will snaffle the lot.

A Life

I never saw the judge
Who sentenced me.

Foreign, I think. Some curt
Three-letter name

Suggesting deserts. No
Jury, no press,

No public interest.
Court officers,

Professionally kind,
Explained the law

Regarding benefit,
Remission, drugs.

I didn't take it in,
The nightmared don't

Study the science of
Dreaming, just wait

For release. Those having
Nothing to wait

For go on waiting (their
Syntax deranged

As their dreams). My prison
Soon smelt of me,

Became familiar as
A bed. I could

Weep in all its corners.
Books, food, were what

You might expect. No view
From the shutters;

That was fitting. Music
Stabbed me; silence

Was offered. The chaplain
Visited, but

Had been gagged. I was glad.
I saw only

The hand of the warder,
Holding my dish.

Looked no further, knowing
If I explored

From wrist up arm to face
What I should find:

The proud, unalterable
Eyes of love.

May 8th: how to recognise it

The tulips have finished their showy conversation.
Night's officers came briefly to report,
And took their heads off.

The limes have the look of someone
Who has been silent a long time,
And is about to say a very good thing.

Roses grow taller, leafier,
Duller. They have star parts;
Like great actors, they hang about humbly in the wings.

On the lawn, daisies sustain their candid
Childish shout. Hippy dandelions are stoned
Out of their golden minds. And always

The rub-a-dub-dub recapitulation
Of grass blades growing. The plum tree is resting
Between blossom and fruit. Like a poker-player,

She doesn't show her hand. Daffodils
Are a matter of graceless brown leaves and rubber bands.
Wallflowers have turned bony.

This is not the shining childhood of spring,
But its homely adolescence, angular, hypothetical.
How one regrets the blue fingertips staggering
Up from the still dank earth.

Neighbours

The Collared couple lived at number one,
In the guttering. They were good neighbours,
Kept an orderly house, the missus was always home.
They might have been R.C. Her tender nape
Bent over her brood was slightly Madonna-ish,
And the three notes they chanted all day, all day,
Some kind of psalm?

Ivy made the gable a high-rise ghetto;
The Blackies at 1b were a racketty lot.
Kept odd hours, zoomed home like motorbikes revving,
Tried to mug the Collareds, at the least excuse
Would scream blue murder, threaten to call the cops.
It was because of them the cat left home.

Our next-door neighbours keep themselves to themselves.
We swap small talk and seedlings over the fence
Sometimes, but not too often. You have to keep
A certain distance.

Two terrorists at large in our neighbourhood
Must have holed up somewhere close. We haven't seen them.
Our neighbours have. *Her*, with her kill,
Standing as if at home on the compost heap,
One foot upraised to pluck. She didn't move,
Outstared them till they backed into the house.
They talk of her yellow eyes, her butcher's poise,
The pigeon bleeding in her taloned fist.

To be a sparrowhawk's neighbour is an honour,
And yet the harmless squabs and fledgling blacks
(Her prey) are neighbours too. We let them be,
And then she guts them for the fluffy brood
She nurtures with the awesome tenderness
We see on television.

                              We don't say this
To our human neighbours, not-quite-friends,
In case they think we're soft. You have to keep
A certain distance.

The Old Lady and the Weather

Raining? Oh dear, you say.
The farmers want it, I correct you,
Look at the garden.
Yes, you say.

Is it fine outside? you ask.
Foggy, I tell you. *There'll be pile-ups*
On motor-ways today.
Oh dear, you say.

Lovely day! you say,
And I, *Rain on the way.*

Why can't you have your own fine indoors weather?
Why must I bring these chills into the house,
When that shape-changer on the other channel
Will have you sooner than you think, you think but never say,
Out in all weathers, ever?

The Poet's Companion

Must be in mint condition, not disposed
To hayfever, headaches, hangovers, hysteria, these being
The Poet's prerogative.

Typing and shorthand desirable. Ability
To function on long walks and in fast trains an advantage.
Must be visible/invisible

At the drop of a dactyl. Should be either
A mobile dictionary, thesaurus and encyclopaedia,
Or have instant access to same.

Cordon bleu and accountancy skills essential,
Also cooking of figures and instant recall of names
Of once-met strangers.

Should keep a good address book. In public will lead
The laughter, applause, the unbearably moving silence.
Must sustain with grace

The role of Muse, with even more grace the existence
Of another eight or so, also camera's curious peeping
When the Poet is reading a particularly

Randy poem about her, or (worse) about someone else.
Ability to endure reproaches for forgetfulness, lack of interest,
Heart, is looked for,

Also instant invention of convincing excuses for what the Poet
Does not want to do, and long-term ability to remember
Precise detail of each.

Must be personable, not beautiful. The Poet
Is not expected to waste time supervising
The Companion. She will bear

Charming, enchanted children, all of them
Variations on the Poet theme, and
Impossibly gifted.

Must travel well, be fluent in the more aesthetic
European languages; must be a Finder
Of nasty scraps of paper

And the miscellany of junk the Poet loses
And needs *this minute, now*. Must be well-read,
Well-earthed, well able

To forget her childhood's grand trajectory,
And sustain with undiminished poise
That saddest dedication: *lastly my wife,*

Who did the typing.

The Receptionist to her Watch

Your job: to wake me with your tiny chime
(*De Camptown Racetrack*) at the proper time.
So what possessed you, that Outpatients day,
While I was holding a shaky hand, to come butting in with your
endless, heartless *doo dah doo dah dey*?

Special

We were special, our class.
Others knew less than us
(More, sometimes), but we were us,
The Clerks of the Weather,
Miss Knowles said.

We knew long words for him,
Our Weather, and had little toys
Like bones for dogs. Weather likes
Pinecones and seaweed,
So we brought them for him
(Or her). When they've decided if
It's boy-weather or girl-weather,
Miss Knowles will tell us,
She said.

Nice thing about Weather is
He knows what he's going to do
Before he does it, and *we* know
What *he* knows. That's why we're special.

I think of him, our Weather, shaggy old dog,
Lying all hairy by the fire of the sun,
Then barking, and shaking snow all over the world,
Or breathing fog at us, sending loony messages
In seaweed and fircones. *Good* dog, Weather.
I'll have a dog just like you when I grow up.

Superannuated Psychiatrist

Old scallyway scapegoat has skedaddled,
Retired at last to bridge and both kinds of bird-watching.
No more suspect phone calls from shady acquaintances,
Anonymous ladies and flush-faced Rotarians.

He could always be blamed when case-notes strayed.
(His MG boot? His mistress's bed? We enjoyed guessing.)
How we shall miss his reliable shiftiness,
Wow and flutter on tape, Wimbledon-fortnight illness,

Dr Macavity life. Dear foxy quack,
I relished your idleness, your improvisations,
Your faith in my powers of you-preservation.
Who will shoulder our errors now?

What of your replacement, the new high flyer,
Smelling of aftershave and ambition? Is that tic
Telling us something his mind will arrive at later?
Meantime, I watch his parentheses. A man so much given

To brackets is hedging his bets.

THREE BRISTOL POEMS

Friends' Meeting House, Frenchay, Bristol

When the doors of the house are shut,
Eyes lidded, mouth closed, nose and ears
Doing their best to idle, fingers allowed out
Only on parole; when the lovely holy distractions,
Safe scaffolding of much-loved formulae,
Have been rubbed away; then the plant
Begins to grow. It is hard to rear,
Rare herb of silence, through which the Word comes.
Three centuries of reticent, meticulous lives
Have naturalised it on this ground.

And the herb is the Vine, savage marauder,
That spreads and climbs unstoppably,
Filling the house, the people, with massing insistent shoots
That leaf through windows and doors, that rocket through
                                  chimneys,
Till flesh melts into walking forms of green,
Trained to the wildness of Vine, which exacts
Such difficult witness; whose work is done
In hopeless places, prisons, workhouses,
In countinghouses of respectable merchants,
In barracks, collieries, sweatshops, in hovels
Of driven and desperate men.

                          It begins here
In the ground of silence.

The Middle Passage

... and the sombre absent presences
Of the Middle Passage, of those
Who never saw Bristol; who were sold
On the Guinea Coast for cloth,
Jet, beads, muskets, spirits, trinkets
And other things accepted by the Moors;
Who were shipped like cattle, the Males
Kept apart from the Females, and handcuffed
(Bristol ships triple such as are sturdy,
With Chains round their Necks);
Who never saw Bristol; who were sold
In Jamaica, Barbados, Antigua, St Kitts,
Virginia, Carolina, to the plantations.

And scudding shipshape back they came,
The little slavers of the Middle Passage,
Marlborough, Tryal, Greyhound, Laughing Sally,
Home to Bristol with their innocent burdens,
Sugar, rum, tobacco, supplied
By the sombre absent presences
Of the Middle Passage, by those
Whom Bristol never saw ...

Reception in Bristol

These men are rich; they buy
Pictures before asking prices.

Their shirts are exquisite; I know instinctively
I must not say so.

Conversations are precisely timed,
Costing so much per word per minute.

Wives are worn small this year, soberly dressed.
Their eyes are wild, but there is no exit.

Schools that encourage music, says the chairman,
Have no hooligans. No one replies.

The photographer is our memento mori.
He takes two sandwiches at once

From the curtseying waitress. There is a crumb
At the corner of his mouth, and he has

To go on somewhere else. He is here to remind us
That in this city Savage died, a prisoner;

That Chatterton poisoned himself in his London garret
Rather than creep back here.

Titania to Bottom

(*for Alistair and Becky*)

You had all the best lines. I
Was the butt, too immortal
To be taken seriously. I don't grudge you
That understated donkey dignity.
It belongs to your condition. Only,
Privately, you should know my passion
Wasn't the hallucination they imagined,
Meddling king and sniggering fairy.

You, Bottom, are what I love. That nose,
Supple, aware; that muzzle, planted out
With stiff, scratchable hairs; those ears,
Lofty as bulrushes, smelling of hay harvest,
Twitching to each subtle electric
Flutter of the brain! Oberon's loving
Was like eating myself—appropriate,
Tasteless, rather debilitating.

But holding you I held the whole
Perishable world, rainfall and nightjar,
Tides, excrement, dandelions, the first foot,
The last pint, high blood pressure, accident, prose.

The sad mechanical drone of enchantment
Finished my dream. I knew what was proper,
Reverted to fairyland's style.

                           But Bottom, Bottom,
How I shook to the shuffle of your mortal heart.

A Toy

(*for Selima Hill*)

Someone made me,
Clothed me, forbade me
To stand, dance, sing,
Do anything
But strut rat-a-tat with my drum

            Dum-dum

Someone made my monkey-body
Ape his look. I cannot move
Until he turns my key

            Rub-a-dub

Uncrucify my stiff bones, someone.
Strip me, free me, let me stand,
Dance, sing

            Rat-a-tat

Play my own tune,
Do my own thing

            Dum

The Two

His are the shifty promise and the sack,
Forcer of entries through chimney and window.

His household cavalry the Horned Ones, and he
The blood-wearer, whose crew runs the night-sky,

Exact and awful as Exocet. Toddlers taste
His sweet bright lips in urban grottoes

Where he distributes his hard-edged toys.
Eat is his name; Eat or Be Eaten.

She is nameless; green her colour,
Green of new grass, or a starling's freckle.
No ceremony calls her. She comes of herself
And no one celebrates. She is
Her own midnight mass.

The Valley of the Shadow

Need not be a valley. Nor is it always life
That quails in the shadow.

Ours was a canal reach, a mooring suitable
For lovers,

Chilly in early April, but serenaded by
Nightingales, patrolled by pheasants,

Made orderly by a birdscarer. Pleasure craft
Lived near the bridge, in sunlight,

Among green-trunked trees. We saw this,
But we also saw the scared bird, love,

Quail and die in the sunlit shadow.

Waiting

The porter blows his nose with two fingers
In a clinical way.

The nurses giggle when they meet. They have permission to do this.
That is how we know they are nurses.

The receptionist addresses the telephone by its Christian name.
She too is part of the inner circle.

There are two consultants. Occasionally they walk the room.
They are never able to speak.

A great many bit-part players, the outpatients
Have come unprepared. No one has told them
That this is a serious play, they have major parts.
They chat about floods in the Severn valley, softly they practise
breathing.

The worst of all, the man on the stretcher, the woman who cannot
walk,
Are the most at ease. They are the ones
Whom the nurses already know. Who smile, and tease,
Knowing they have reached the last act.

Word Games

1. COMFORTABLE WORDS

'"Never mind," he said, "we'll get the solution tomorrow."'
Elma Mitchell: *Winter in Lodgings*.

When you understand that a river is a flower
You have begun. Friday, of course, is a man,
And a duck means nothing. Victim of gin
Is not an alcoholic, nor revolutionary
Political. Cardinals, favourite standbys,
Are always news. The Mayfair Railway's wiry,
And the 6.50's found in the first three villains.
Night's a dark deranged thing. Possibly, we hear,
Perhaps, can be, are warnings; damaged isn't serious.

He doesn't have to make dying
As hard as this. I've seen how easy-going
He is with the old, the infirm, letting them drift
Unbothered away, like a bleached leaf dropping.
If he can be so kind, why must he prise
My baby's body apart like butcher's meat?
I mustn't think too much. The doctor said so.
But she is broken by successive spasms,
Changed to this thing, squinting, deranged.

The words are not really cross,
Only pretending. The answer will come
In tomorrow's paper. There is nothing here
That won't in the end be solved.
(The answer to a mix-up (8): *solution*.)

But here is also where my little boy
Strains hardly back to me, and my baby
Leaves me for ever. There can be nothing
Worse than this, and this is now,
And I am here inside it. I shall never
Leave this place. (The final exit? (6,4):
Death's door.)

                    This one's hard.
I am familiar with his usual clues,
I know his mind, as if we danced
Kindly together. I think of him
As a friend, tweedy, pipe-smoking,
With a faithful sort of dog—retriever,
Labrador, perhaps. When he's contrived
Some tricky pun I'll just manage to crack
He smiles in my mind: *There, Sweetheart,
I put that in for you.* (Castle I'd reconstruct
To discover local languages (8):

        Dialects.) My baby's local language
    Is anguish. Shrieks are all she says.
    I pray, Frank pays; neither does any good.
    Only the reliable riddle that comes each morning,
    Its answer the day after. (More
    And more cavalry casualties? (8,6):
    Mounting losses.) Although it comforts,
    Each answer bears my darling's dying too.
    Money is nothing, Frank said. Second opinion,
    Trained nurse night and day, whatever
    Does any good. He is so good to me.
    Always the gentleman, knowing I don't much fancy
    That sort of thing.

(Wormwood that can bring joy
To a maiden's heart? (4,4):
Lad's love.) A hard game, yes, but
A fair one. No syllable is meaningless,
The coding is consistent. Down is easier,
Always; helps with Across, is necessary
For working out the pattern. I couldn't crochet
This crossword comforter without my Down.
(Implement satisfied consumer demand,
But not in time (3,4)). I'll need a while

To puzzle that one out.

                        And meantime
Down, Down she goes, my darling.

Note: Answer to last clue—*too late.*

2. NECK-VERSE

Armour of phrase disarms despair;
Ancestral patchwork plasters. Someone else
Was wounded here and stitched a turn to fit
The later maimed. I cherish
A cat's cradle of country proverbs,
Homely as singin' hinnies, handy as hankies.
Not hard equivocal wisdom for grand folk,
But reassuring halloos from the past:
We have been here before you, pet!

My kitchen prescriptions:
For Resignation:
You can't get feathers off the cat.

To take the ache out of Age:
He's seen a few Easter Sundays.

For the different ways menfolk are difficult:
Cross-grained: *He's got his braces twisted.*
Stingy: *He'd kill a louse for the hide and tallow.*
Impossible, like mine: *Awkward as Dick's hatband.*
Went three times round the crown
And wouldn't tie a bow.

Hysteria has many cues; its bubble
Needs pricking. After Effort:
It's all over now, and the child's name's Anthony.
To bypass weepy Thanks: *That'll be ninepence,*
Or *Keep your seats, there's no collection.*

For Last Ditch Stands: *That's me,*
And my dog's at Tow Law.

And O, for how it should be, could have been,
I have two simples: *As easy*
As me granny's old shoe, and
All in together, like the folks at Shields.

Too often, though, just the longing
For freedom, a fresh start:
I wish I was married and living at Jarrow.

I know what they'll say of me: *she brought*
Her pigs to a poor market in the end. Yes,
That'll be what it'll be. And to comfort me,
Cheer up, hinny, it's nobody's neck.

But that's not true. It is some body's neck.
It's mine.

Neck Verse: the first verse of psalm 51, so called because it was the trial verse of
those who claimed Benefit of Clergy. If a condemned person was able to read
this verse (thus originally showing that he was ordained, and therefore exempt
from trial by a secular court), he had saved his neck. This privilege was later
extended to anyone who could read and write, or even who knew the psalm's
first verse by heart. It was abolished in 1827.

Awkward Subject

The light is wonderful, he says. Not light
For house-agents, certainly. They avoid
November shots, when wisped and bony trees
Throw a disturbing shade on property.

Stand there. Just a bit further. Don't look at the dog.
My casual adaptation to the place
(One hand in pocket, right knee slightly bent)
May not be what I mean, but is in danger
Of immortality.

              I feel my teeth support me
Against my inner lip; face him with all my skin.
Sensing my misery, *Would you rather smile?*
He asks. And break the lens, I hope. Words are my element.
Photograph them.

Programmed

Their idea of truth is yesterday's weather.
They track it through slots in clouds
Down a freezing hospital garden.

His idea of truth is what was said
Before, in unscripted rehearsal. But the words he wants
Weren't mine. He committed them.

My truth is the one that really was
(I think). The chair goes here, not here.
And those distressful lights, do they represent

The just understatement of daylight?
I try to pin down the homely fact
Of what happened, was felt.

The reproachful murmur of poems reminds me
They are not compromised. But at each take
Something diminishes.

Only body, with its helpless accuracy,
When the phone rings, recovers unprompted
The hunch and duck of slavery,
Remembers the words.

Notes at a Photographic Exhibition

JULIA MARGARET CAMERON: CALL AND I FOLLOW, I FOLLOW—LET ME DIE
(c. 1867).

I see in women's faces the desire
For sacrifice. The unprotected eye,
Hair rippling helplessly, the mouth
In glowing readiness to take what comes —
A death, a kiss.

TONY RAY-JONES: ERNIE CAGNOLATTI AND GRANDSON, 1971

This, I guess, is what a jazzman
Wants in the end. Kid with a sax,
Grandson, more of a black than me,
With a tear in his pants, but plays
A bigger instrument, going my way,
But gonna go way way further . . .

TONY RAY-JONES: BILLIE PIERCE, NEW ORLEANS, 1971

My shoulder-straps show. I don't care
My age shows. I don't care.
Sadness shows. I don't care.

I am what I am: old woman
Tired, glad to sit down, weepy-eyed.
Worked hard, sung hard, lived hard.
Make what you can of it. You're welcome.

EDWARD WESTON: ON ROUTE US 61, MISSISSIPPI (1941)

One day this truck'll be out of date,
These gas pumps too. Shell
Will probably stick around, maybe
There'll still be Toastmasters. But Ole Missus
Won't stay under this Toastmaster, nor will you
Be able to take this swollen me, smiling, black,
Offering you something, with a hopeful look,
And a door in my skirt.

EDWARD WESTON: FARM HOUSE IN NEW JERSEY, 1941

Look close. This is not comfortable country.
For the folk who live here, depression
Is not a state of mind.
Nothing here is picturesque, neither trees,
Nor boarded windows, nor the shack
In the yard. The invisible people
Are avoiding each other's eyes. We could tell them
That hope is on its way. Its name is War.

AGNES B WARBURG: OÙ SONT LES NEIGES D'ANTAN?

It's a matter of angles and implications.
Why, mademoiselle, do you choose not to reveal
My face? Because it might be smiling?
Why do you emphasise the empty chairs?
As it happens, I like to sit by myself.
Does anyone want snow
To last for ever?

62

FREDERICK H EVANS: FREDERICK HOLLAND DAY

This is the me you might see in the street,
Taken by my friend, another
Photographer Fred. Closed mouth, lensed eyes,
Reticent beard. You can't be sure of me,
Or anything. That is my message;
At least, it's what I told Fred my message is.

FREDERICK HOLLAND DAY: THE CRUCIFIXION

I am the man who was lifted up,
And came down again on the same day,
Getting ahead of Christ. Don't suppose it was easy.
I starved six months for this
Skeletal effect, grew my hair, planned
My crucifixion to the last painted detail.
The nails are counterfeit, but as you see my arms
Are genuine. I took the photograph, too,
Making it easy for the world to believe in me.

ROGER FENTON (WATERFALL IN WOOD)

I gave this piece no name. As barrister
And man of words, I had my silent reasons.
De minimis non curat lex. It is the trifles here,
Too small for words, that matter.
So many leaves, more leaves than any painter
Could ever show, all witness to themselves.
The light stalks through the air and catches water,
And growing things. The rule of law
Has been here, interposed a bridge, and left
A world of wildness, world not needing word.